# Who Am I?

By Liza Charlesworth

ISBN: 978-1-339-02680-0

Art Director: Tannaz Fassihi; Designer: Tanya Chernyak
Photos © Getty Images.
Copyright © Liza Charlesworth. All rights reserved. Published by Scholastic Inc.

3  4  5  6  7  8  9  10   68   32  31  30  29  28  27  26  25  24

Printed in Jiaxing, China. First printing, August 2023.

**SCHOLASTIC**

I'm red with 4 legs.
I can stand on a rock.
Who am I? I'm a fox!

It's fun to hop and hop.
It's fun to swim in a bog.
Who am I? I'm a frog!

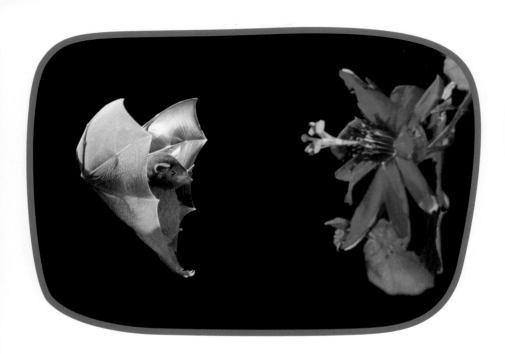

I'm tan and can flap.
I snack on plants and bugs.
Who am I? I'm a bat!

It's fun to sit in the mud.
I do not say, "Yuck!"
Who am I? I'm a pig!

Am I big? Yes!
I'm fast in the grass.
Who am I? I'm a ram!

I'm not as big as a ram.
I'm red with black spots.
Who am I? I'm a bug!

I'm a kid's best pal.
It's fun to say, "RUFF!"
Who am I? I'm a dog!